IMAGINE

BELIEVE IN THE POWER OF A DREAM

FRANK DAMAZIO

PUBLISHED BY CITY CHRISTIAN PUBLISHING
9200 NE Fremont, Portland, Oregon 97220

City Christian Publishing is a ministry of City Bible Church and is dedicated to serving the local church and its leaders through the production and distribution of quality equipping resources. It is our prayer that these materials, proven in the context of the local church, will equip leaders in exalting the Lord and extending His kingdom.

For a free catalog of additional resources from City Christian Publishing, please call 1-800-777-6057 or visit our web site at www.CityChristianPublishing.com.

Imagine
ISBN 13: 978-1-59383-037-3
ISBN 10: 1-59383-037-8

Cover, Interior designed and typeset by City Christian Publishing.

First Edition, July 2006

Printed in the United States of America

Contents

Chapter 1: Imagine is a Dream Word 5

Chapter 2: Imagine is a Faith Word 21

Chapter 3: Imagine is a God-Thought 35

Chapter 4: Imagine is a Holy Spirit Word 55

Chapter 5: Imagine is a Vision Word 71

Chapter 6: Imagine is a Miracle Word 99

   Appendix 111

   Endnotes 117

Chapter 1

Imagine is a Dream Word

Walt and Art had been good friends for many years and Walt was eager to show Art his latest dream. He drove Art out of the city and down country roads, through fields and orange groves before finally stopping. Walking through the orange groves, he spoke excitedly of his dream for this empty orange grove. "I'm going to build a family fun park here. Over there is going to be the merry-go-round and over here the roller coaster. Can you see it?" But Art couldn't see it. All he could see was barren land in the middle of nowhere. Walt said, "I've bought this land and I'm going to build here, but you need to buy up the land over there and build some hotels and restaurants for all the people coming to the fun park. That land will be worth millions. Can you see it?" But Art couldn't see it.

Years later Art stood looking at Disneyland, the dream that his friend Walt had built, and calculated how much that dream was now worth. He looked at the land he had walked and estimated the dream had cost him $3 million per step for every step he took as he walked unseeing through Walt's dream. He lost millions because he couldn't see the invisible dream and Walt Disney made billions because he could. [1]

Walt Disney is known for imagining and for acting on what he imagined. How many times have you heard someone say, "Can you imagine...?" "Imagine that!" Children have such great imaginations, yet by the time they become adults they lose that ability to believe the possibilities that lie around them. They allow life to put a lid on their minds and spirits.

I want to get you to take that lid off your spirit. I want to get you to move into a new realm of seeing things that maybe you don't see right now. I want you to begin to challenge the assumptions you have made about life and about yourself. We all make assumptions about life, about God, and about our future, and we accept these assumptions as truth, as reality, and we don't go beyond them. We never question these assumptions or step beyond their limits. Today you need to begin to challenge them.

Divine interruptions challenge life assumptions

Solomon had some assumptions about life. He assumed that life was progressing according to his pre-determined plan. He was king and he probably had lots of ideas in his mind as to what he wanted to do now that he had the power and resources to do them, then God interrupted him. God appeared to Solomon in a dream one night and changed Solomon's life *(1 Kings 3:5)*.

This is the divine interruption principle. You're going along in life and think you've pretty much got things planned and you know where you are going. Maybe you think you've got your life plans worked out and know where you are going and then comes the divine interruption. God comes. God interrupts your life.

It could be a crossroads time or a pivotal point. It could be an encounter with God through fasting and prayer as God begins to stir things within your spirit. It could be an encounter with God in a church service as the Holy Spirit begins to speak with you and open your heart in an area of your life. You are going about daily life and before you know it, you're having a divine interruption.

God begins to speak with you about things you hadn't been thinking about. He begins to direct your steps towards places you were not heading. He begins to open your mind to ideas you hadn't had before. Before you know it, your life has been interrupted because God is encountering you to take you to new places and to imagine new things.

God came to Solomon in a dream. We all have dreams. Some come from eating too much pizza or watching strange movies just before you go to bed. Those aren't the dreams I'm referring to. I'm talking about a dream that is given by God.

It is a dream that you see with wide-open eyes, a dream that comes in the flash of a moment, a dream that is deposited in your spirit in a split-second. This is a dream that changes your life so you can never go back to the way you were. When God drops a dream in your heart, your life has been divinely interrupted and it will never be the same.

Ask what I should give you

Imagine God coming to you and saying, "Ask what I should give you and I'll do it." That shouldn't take too much imagining because we can read about what happened when God did it. This isn't an obscure event that happened only to Solomon. Several times in the Bible, God speaks to a person, either directly or through someone else, and says, "Ask whatever you want and I'll give it to you." *(Matthew 21:22; Mark 11:24; John 14:13; John 15:16; John 16:23; 1 John 3:22; 1 John 5:15; 1 Kings 3:5)*

Of course, our mind immediately puts a limit on that. "He'll give up to this much. There's no way He would really give me anything I want." We can joke about this or we can get serious and say, "Wouldn't it be awesome if I could ask anything that I wanted that would be focused on the kingdom of God, on glorifying the Lord and making an impact on people's lives?" Charles Finney said, "We are to ask earnestly, to ask largely, to ask perseveringly, in order that we may honor and glorify him." [2]

If you could ask God for anything, what would you ask? What limitations do you put on your requests? Are you limited by what you think God will answer? Are you limited by how much you think He has? What assumptions do you have that affect your limitations? Challenge your assumptions! Get out of the box of your limitations.

What is your box?

We live in a box in every area of life—physically, mentally, emotionally, spiritually and financially. We let lines be drawn around us that box us in and limit what we can imagine.

Bill Gates knew how to imagine. Bill Gates is a Harvard dropout and a techno-geek. Why did he drop out? He saw something. The result of what he saw is the Microsoft Corporation with 60,000 employees and a personal net worth of $45 billion. What did he see? He saw a world of computers with no limits to the possibilities. He allowed no lines to limit what he could imagine, no lines to box him in. He didn't allow his vision to be limited by perceived reality. He challenged the assumptions.

When he built his own home, he allowed his imagination to go beyond the normal and created a "smart house." As you walk through the door, the lights come on and follow you from room to room, turning on as you enter and off as you leave. That's every parents' dream! Just think, never coming home again to find every light in the house on and nobody home. You assume that you can listen to music while you are in your living room or your bedroom, but how about your pool? Challenge the assumptions! You put your favorite CD on in the living room, but then you decide to take a swim in the pool. The music follows you down to your bedroom where you change clothes, along the hall to the pool and even into the deep end of the pool as you dive in. Not bad! [3]

Art Linkletter had assumptions about the desolate orchard that Walt Disney showed him. He assumed it was valueless and empty of opportunity. But Walt Disney challenged the assumptions. He saw a door where there was none and went through it. Art couldn't see so he drew back and missed an opportunity which could have changed his future.

If you can't see it before it exists, you will never see it in reality. If you can't imagine it, you draw back and miss the possibilities. If you assume it will never be, you can't imagine it.

The Power of Imagining

The power of imagining did not originate with man. It's a God-word. It is part of the very nature of God. What is the first thing the Bible tells us about God? What did He do "in the beginning"? He made everything and everything that God made He saw first. All that was invisible was in the heart of God before it ever became visible for man to enjoy. God could see it all. He looked at emptiness and saw a planet, animals, plants and man. God saw them and He made them reality.

Why is imagining so important?

God put in every individual the power of imagining, which gives birth to vision. Without imagining, you can't see potential in front of you. Without imagining you only look at things that are there. But when you begin to imagine what God might do, you begin to see beyond.

I want to motivate you to ask. I cannot promise what answer you will receive. I cannot dictate to God

"Imagination is more important than knowledge. For knowledge is limited to all we know and understand, while imagination embraces all there ever will be to know and understand."

—*Albert Einstein*

how big your dream should be. I cannot dictate to the invisible kingdom of God anything about your life. That's between you and God. But there is one thing that I can do. I can tell you to ask big. I can tell you to take the lid off your imagining and take a risk. Take a chance. Move into the realm of imagining, the realm of faith. Move into the realm of miracles, the realm of the supernatural. As long as you live in the realm of the natural, the realm of rational reasoning, you never begin to dream.

Definition of imagine

The word imagine means a form of vivid, powerful images of something not present to your senses. You can't grasp it with all your natural faculties. You have to go beyond that. It's not yet present to the senses. Why? Because it is imagination. It is the non-tangible, the unreal. The Bible's way of saying "imagine" is the simple word "faith". *(Hebrews 11:1-2)*

Definition of dreams

What is a dream? A dream is a visionary creation that works into the imagination of a person. It is a future hope or desire that lives inside you. Your mind picks up on your imagination and begins to meditate on it. Your thoughts begin to reflect and dwell on what is inside as your spirit feeds your mind its hopes and desires.

Dreams are the goals and vision that fire your heart and saturate your soul. What fires your heart? What makes you passionate? For Walt Disney it was seeing a place where families could come for fun. For Bill Gates it is shaping the way people live. What stirs passion in you?

Encourage people to dream

Our world often calls dreamers space cadets. It says they live in unreality. A person with a vivid imagination is seen as a person who needs to get in touch with reality. Society tries to force them to become just like every other non-dreamer—unhappy, unfulfilled, working a boring job and worrying only about getting food on the table. It shrinks them back down to the level of the ordinary instead of saying to them, "That's an awesome idea. That might work. Keep thinking about it because God could enlarge your world to fit you into that."

What do you do when people start dreaming out loud in front of you? When the Walt Disneys in your life begin to verbalize their imaginings, do you encourage them or belittle their dreams?

Passion fruit

Have you heard of the passion fruit? It's a small egg-shaped fruit. Don't you wish it could live up to its name? You eat passion fruit and you get passion. Every morning on the way to work you could reach over, break open the lunch pail and eat your quota of passion fruit for the day. All of a sudden—you're passionate! Don't you wish it were that easy?! How about vision fruit? Just buy this fruit, eat it and start seeing visions. Imagine fruit? You eat that one and you get brand new thoughts and ideas. If only it were that easy! Yet in some ways, it is. The fruit of the Spirit is faith and if you have faith, you begin to see things. You begin to dream new dreams.

A dreamer is someone who lives in the world of imagination. A visionary lives in the world of dreams and imagination yet that world becomes reality to them. When they try to tell someone about the reality, it can sound like a fantasy. Young Jim was staring out the window when his mother came to tuck him into bed. She asked him what he was doing. Very simply he spoke his dream into reality, "Looking at the moon. You know, one day I'm going to walk on the moon." Fantasy, unreality. Yet 32 years later that fantasy, that unreal dream, became reality as James Irwin stepped onto the moon.

A dreamer is one who sees the future as if it is already here. The dream overtakes your thought and your thought overtakes your emotion and your emotion gets into your feet and hands and you start living it out. God gives you the ability to see the future as if it is already here. T.E. Lawrence once said, "All men dream, but not equally. Those who dream by night in the dusty recesses of their minds wake in the day to find that it was vanity: but the dreamers of the day are dangerous men, for they may act their dreams with open eyes, to make it possible. This I did." [4] Are you a dreamer of the night who never lives your dreams into reality or a dreamer of the day who acts upon your dream?

Are you still breathing?

Imagine. *Imagine—at my age?* Yes, imagine at your age! Imagine someone congratulating you on your 90th birthday and on your new baby. *Baby? Ninety years old?* Sarah's response was the same as yours would be, "Yeah right! That's a good one! Ha ha!" She sat in her tent, listening to the conversation outside and laughed, only to hear the angel say, "I hear you laughing. It is going to happen and you will name your child "Isaac," which means "laughter."

Think about it. When you start saying, "I'm too old. I don't have the resources. My past prevents me. I can't change anything." Those are the assumptions of the devil and those are lies. As long as you are breathing, there is no limit on your imagining. If you have a pulse, you have the power of imagining. You can imagine.

The Boll Weevil Principle:
Dreams come after a crisis

> And the Lord said to Abram, after Lot had separated from him: 'Lift your eyes now and look from the place where you are—northward, southward, eastward and westward; for all the land which you see I give to you and your descendants forever.' (Genesis 13:14-15)

There is a pivotal point in your life. You hit the wall. This is an opportune time for a dream or vision to be born. This is the Boll Weevil Principle.

If you drive through a small town called Enterprise, Alabama, you'll find a statue of a woman holding a small fountain over her head with a boll weevil on top. There are monuments to soldiers, to politicians, to artists—but to a bug? Who builds a monument to a bug, a destructive bug that devastates crops?

In 1915 the boll weevil immigrated into Alabama from Mexico and began a rampage of destruction. By 1918 farmers were losing entire crops to this devastating insect and they knew something had to be done. If they didn't solve this problem, they were finished. One man allowed his imagination to soar. H.M. Sessions realized that the future of the town lay with a different crop, and he began to try to convince others of the reality of his dream. It took him a year to find someone who would listen and back his plan to plant peanuts. When his peanut crop proved successful, all the other farmers quickly followed his example, not only saving their town but changing the economy of their county.

Everybody has boll weevil times in their life. Things are at a dead end. The problems facing them are huge. But if you have eyes to see, it is the beginning of a new vision. It is the opening of a new open door with a great future.

The Abraham Principle:
Start dreaming where you are

Genesis 13 tells of a difficult time for Abraham. Lot, his nephew, had packed his bags and left. After all Abraham had done for him, treating him like a son, he had washed his hands of their relationship and walked out. God said, "Abraham, what's the matter?" "I'm hurting, God. I'm so discouraged. My family has left and I'm alone in a strange country."

God tells Abraham to "Lift up your eyes and look from the place where you are." We always want to wait until things are perfect. We want to get to the top of the mountain and then look. But God says, "Look from where you are right now." We may not feel like looking, but if we listen, we can hear God say, "Lift up your eyes and look north, south, east and west from right here because I'm going to give you this land." We need to lift up our spiritual eyes and see.

When you get up in the middle of the night, you stumble across the floor with your hands stretched out to prevent you from bumping into things. You don't confidently stride across the room and out the door. Why? You can't see. It's the same in the spiritual. If you can't see, you stumble and fall. You move hesitantly and fearfully. No one can move into the future or toward a goal unless they can see it.

Vision is an awesome thing. Without vision, you don't move confidently. You don't move with commitment. You don't make the necessary adjustments to reach your goal if you can't see where you are going. Vision is critical for success.

Open your spiritual eyes

Allow God to open your eyes so that you can imagine, dream, see, envision. God wants us to go far past where we are, to a new level in Him, a new level in our personal lives, a new level in our families, jobs, businesses, relationships.

Imagine! Imagine what you would do if resources were not a problem. Imagine what you would do if you could forget the failures of the past and move ahead into the future. Imagine what you would do if you would let go of the baggage from the past. Imagine!

What is God speaking to your heart? What is the hope that lies deep within you, the dream that whispers into your heart as you lie in bed at night? The beginning of your ability to imagine is to ask God for His dream and His will for your life.

Prayer for Vision

Lord, give me a dream. Give me a vision. I'm not too young to do your will. I'm not too old to begin another chapter of imagining. Give me a dream and a vision for today. Don't let me rest on the dreams of the past that have already been fulfilled but to up the ante and step into another level of the dream, another part to the vision.

Chapter 2

Imagine is a Faith Word

W hen Charles Kettering was research head of General Motors and wanted a problem solved, he would call his workers into the meeting room. Outside the room would be a table with a sign prominently displayed: "Leave slide rules here." He had found that in the middle of a brainstorming session when one person would be "imagining"—thinking outside the box—someone else would grab a slide rule, make some calculations, and announce, "You can't do that." [1] They would get so locked into reality they couldn't see the possibilities.

Living the invisible

Imagining is not just seeing the invisible, but living the invisible through faith. It is living in a realm where reality seems to say one thing and your dream another. Faith is the realm that does not agree with your senses. It is the realm that seems to contradict reality.

This is where we get locked up and put in a box. We want our reasoning to be the guide of our life, but reasoning doesn't always cooperate when you move into faith. Your mind and rational thinking can be in direct contradiction to what God says. God says, "Do this" and our mind immediately responds, "There's no way! I can't go there. I can't do that. I don't have the ability. I don't have the resources. It doesn't make any sense!" We can't imagine it.

Have a wise foundation

Some people live so far off the ground that their imaginings need to be reined in. But for most people, that's not the case. Most people allow reality to dictate their dreams instead of allowing their dreams to give life to a new reality. Yes, we need a balance to reality and dreams, but the balance is not to "get real." It is to get character, get good foundations, get wisdom. If you act in contradiction to godly character or biblical foundations or wise counsel, you will end up with problems. So get godly character that is built on biblical foundations and lived through wise counsel. Then begin to imagine.

You have the ability to dream

In you are seeds of greatness, dream-seeds of visions that will take you beyond your frustration and discouragement, beyond your lack of esteem and feeling of inferiority. God can help you. You do not have to live down to the defeatist words from your past. You do not have to live in agreement with the taunts that you will never live up to your potential, that you have no potential to live up to, that you are doomed for failure.

God is for you. He will lift you up. He will give you a promise and a dream. You might be running into wall after wall. You may be doing more crawling on your knees than walking on your feet. I'm telling you right now to lift your eyes and see. Your life is meant for more than this. God is for you. God is with you. There is more for your life than what you are experiencing. God is not discouraged with you. He will forgive you, cleanse you and put you on your feet again. He is a good God. Lift up your eyes and go for what God wants to do in your life.

The greatest theft in town

The greatest theft that took place in your city this weekend was not a bank robbery. It wasn't stolen cars or home burglaries or identity theft. The greatest theft that goes on every day in our world is the enemy stealing the dream from someone's heart. When the devil steals your ability to imagine, he has stolen something from you that is worth more than millions. He has stolen something far more precious than money. It is that part of Himself that God put in you that allows you to imagine and to dream.

God has a dream for your life. He has a word for you. He has a future for you. God has something great in store for you. You are not too old to believe and imagine. There have been people in their 70s, 80s and 90s who didn't allow their age to limit their ability to imagine, and they accomplished some of the greatest things of their lives in their latter years. Have you already resigned from life? Do you think that at 50 or 60 or 70 your life is over and there's not much left to do? There's so much more ahead for you! There is so much more that God wants to do in you. There is so much more that He could do through you. But if you are already dead, just walk out the door and fall into a hole somewhere. If you're already dead and all we're waiting for is a funeral, then just go drop yourself into a hole and wait for someone to cover you up. But if you have breath in your lungs, God can use you.

Faith is the foundation

Every person needs to build in their lives a foundation for the dream that God has given them. That foundation is the starting point for everyone to imagine, to see, to lift up their eyes and grasp God's desire for their future. So what is that foundation? Faith.

"Now faith is the substance of things hoped for, the evidence of things not seen." *(Hebrews 11:1)*

This verse gives us the Bible definition of faith. It is one simple phrase that you need to put into your spirit. *Faith is the substance.* Faith is the substance of things hoped for. I see you pulling out your slide rule, "That doesn't make sense. That's not reality. If something is hoped for, there's no substance to it. It's not real yet."

Wait a minute with that slide rule. God's not done with His definition yet. He goes on to say that faith is the "evidence of things not seen." That is not reality to us, yet to God that is a very simple reality. Faith is the substance of things hoped for, the evidence of things not seen. Some other interpretations include:

Faith is the assurance of things hoped for *(American Standard Version).*

Faith is the confident assurance of that for which we hope (*Weymouth*).

Faith forms a solid ground for what is hoped for (*Berkley*).

Faith is the title deed of things hoped for (*Mon*).

Faith gives substance to our hope (*New English Bible*).

Faith is the subtle assurance of the things you don't have but that are coming. With faith you form a solid ground to build your hope on. You build a solid foundation for the invisible, acting as if you have it when it has not yet been created.

Faith is a title deed

Faith is the title deed to the things of the future. A title deed is a proof of ownership. Imagine you're sitting on the bus and an elderly gentleman gets on and sits next to you. He shoots the breeze for awhile and then hands you a piece of paper as he stands up to leave. "What's this?" "That's a title deed to a car," he tells you. "That piece of paper means that you now own a brand new Hummer. I own the company and I'm designing a brand-new model that surpasses all the other ones ever built. It will be the best car ever. There's just one thing you need to understand. I have the designs in my head but we haven't begun building them yet. We're going to begin production soon and the first one off the assembly line is yours. That title deed proves it."

Would you throw the piece of paper away as valueless? Or would you hang onto it and tell everyone, "I've got a Hummer! Top of the line! Latest model, straight off the assembly line!" Do you have the car? "Well, not really. I mean I do own the car, but I don't have the car." You have the title deed for a car that is not yet real. So what good is the title deed? You hang onto it, keep it, and one day you walk into the factory and point to the car coming off the line and say, "That's mine." They put the key in your hands and the substance of that title deed becomes real and you drive off in it.

Zacharias and the title deed

That "unbelievable" look in your eyes is the same look Zacharias had when an angel suddenly appeared right in front of him while he was at work. *A baby? A boy?* "Yeah right. We aren't exactly in the prime of life right now. Our friends are already having grandkids and now you're saying we're having our first kid? I don't think so. Not real!" He pulls out the slide rule and starts looking at reality. "I don't believe. It can't be. It's impossible. What? You have a birth certificate with his name on it? John? This is just a piece of paper. It doesn't mean anything. I'll tell you what's real. I'm old and my wife—let's just say she's not exactly young anymore. You expect me to walk out of here and tell her she's going to get pregnant just because an angel said it? Maybe you aren't an angel. Maybe the grape juice I had for breakfast was a little fermented. You can't be real and a baby named John can't be real."

One thing to remember about arguing with God—you can't win. The angel finally got fed up with Zack and said, "Alright, I'm done with you. No more arguing. Your mouth is zipped until the baby is born. You aren't able to speak faith? You won't be able to speak at all. *Zip.* Done."

Sometimes we try to confess ourselves right out of the will of God. We make unbelieving statements and unbelieving declarations. We argue with God about what His will is. We argue the greatness of His word and confess ourselves right out what He wants to do.

What do you do when your dream is so different you can't talk about it? What do you do when you can't even confess it to yourself? There are many people like that in the Bible. From beginning to end, you find God coming to people and saying, "Here's the title deed for your victory" and they would stare back and say, "Huh?"

Gideon and the title deed

Look at Gideon. He didn't have a chance. He had 300 men against an army that looked like a plague of locusts spread across the valley. Everywhere you looked there were tents and camels and men. You couldn't even see the floor of the valley for the multitude of soldiers down there. And Gideon had 300 men looking over his shoulder saying, "We're attacking *that!?*"

God is saying, "Here's the title deed for your victory" and Gideon can't see it. All he can see when he closes his eyes is the massive army surrounding his puny little group. He can't see past reality into the realm of the supernatural. So God sends him down to hear someone who does see the deed.

Two of the enemy soldiers are talking, "I had a dream. An ordinary loaf of bread came rolling down that hill right there and hit this tent and leveled it. That insignificant object bowled over and devastated something hundreds of times its size." As Gideon listens, the other soldier responds in fear, "That little loaf of bread is Gideon and his armies. They're going to wipe us out." He had more faith than Gideon had! But Gideon heard and responded. He realized that the title deed is a guarantee of the promise.

"For we walk by faith, not by sight."

—*2 Corinthians 5:7*

Six faith declarations

Faith is the substance, the confidence and the substructure of things we hope for.

Faith gives us confidence. It is an assurance. Faith has to be as real to you as something you can touch if you want to move into the realm of the invisible and supernatural.

Faith enables us to treat dreams as reality.

Faith goes into the future and brings dreams back as reality.

It looks into the future and sees what is real there and brings it into the present and begins to act upon that reality.

Faith sees the invisible and receives the impossible.

Faith opens our eyes to visualize things that haven't happened. Faith opens our arms to receive things that seem impossible.

Faith perceives as real fact what is not revealed to the senses.

Our senses argue that something is not there, but faith accepts it as though it is. Faith believes the word of God is more real than what can be seen or touched in the natural.

Faith is to believe what we do not see and the reward of this faith is to see what we believe.

Our natural eyes must line up with our faith eyes. As we begin to see the answer in faith, we begin to look for it in the natural world around us.

Faith is the power that creates things out of nothing.

This is mindboggling. Faith does not need all the elements you may think are needed in order for a dream to be fulfilled. Faith creates things out of nothing. Hebrews 11:3 says, "By faith we understand that the worlds were framed by the word of God, so that the things which are seen were not made of things which are visible." Faith moves into the realm that doesn't have the tangibles and the visibles. R.C.H. Lenski said it this way in his commentary: "By means of faith we understand that the eons have been framed by means of God's uttered word so that what is seen has come to be, not out of things that appear." God speaks and where nothing was, something exists.

Prayer for Faith

Lord, give me faith for the dream. Give me faith to believe that You are the God of the Bible and that You never change. Give me faith to act upon the word You have spoken into my life. Give me faith to live the reality of Your word in spite of what I see around me, trusting that You are greater than what my eye sees or my ears hear.

Chapter 3

Imagine is a God-Thought

> *'For My thoughts are not your thoughts, nor are your ways My ways,' says the Lord. 'For as the heavens are higher than the earth, so are My ways higher than your ways, and My thoughts than your thoughts.' (Isaiah 55:8-9)*

God thinks differently about our lives than we do. He thinks differently about our future than we think. He thinks differently about His promises and what He would like to put into our hands. God's thoughts are higher than our thoughts as much as the heavens are higher than the earth. That's a big gap!

Think higher thoughts

In Philippians 3:12, Paul says, "I press toward the mark for the prize of the high calling of God in Christ Jesus." It's a high call, a high thought. Yet many people aim toward a "low call," an inferior target. They have lower thoughts, lower dreams, and lower visions.

The Bible, quickened through the Holy Spirit, pushes our thoughts higher. The presence of God invades our lives and pushes us to go higher. God begins to pour into our hearts and minds that we are overcomers. We are more than conquerors. We can break these habits. We can do great things. Through God we are mighty men and women of valor.

The Word of the Lord comes in and stirs us to imagine, to believe what God says, and to raise our vision to His vision. Rise up and take what is yours. Don't just sit back and allow life to pass by. Get up and pursue the vision that God has placed in your heart.

You may have forgotten the dream you used to have, but God hasn't. You may not believe in the dream anymore, but He does. He believes in the dream and He believes in you. He has been and is working on you and the dream all the time. Many years may have passed since you first began to dream the dream. You may have lost many precious things. You may have lost hope. The dream may have faded from delay after delay. Mark this down—it's not over yet!

God's thoughts toward you

'For I know the thoughts that I think toward you', says the Lord, 'thoughts of peace and not of evil, to give you a future and a hope.' (Jeremiah 29:11)

What are God's thoughts toward us? Wouldn't it be awesome to put on earphones and begin to listen to a recording of God's thoughts toward you right now?

Have you ever been sitting next to someone on the bus or on a plane who was listening to music on earphones? You can't hear anything, but their head is bobbing, their mouth is moving to words you can't hear and their whole body is in synch with an un-heard beat. They look ridiculous. You sit there and laugh at them because their actions are out of synch with the world around them and they look weird. But if you could hear what they were hearing, you would probably be doing the same thing.

That's the way it is with the thoughts of God. If you start hearing the thoughts of God and hearing what the Lord wants to do in and through you, you will start moving differently. You will begin to respond differently, walk differently, and talk differently. You will be living in a different realm, a realm of God-thoughts.

Thoughts of peace

God says that His thoughts toward us are thoughts of peace. The Hebrew word for peace is often translated as health, wholeness and success. God says, "I'm thinking of you with thoughts that would bring you wholeness and health and success in your journey and achievement for your life. My thoughts are not evil, but thoughts of a good future and hope."

Look at Psalm 139:17: "How precious and weighty also are your thoughts to me, O God! How vast is the sum of them!" [1]

How long has it been since you had a penetrating, lifting-up-and-getting-on-with-it thought from God? How long has it been since a thought so hit you that it changed the way you lived? How long since you had a thought that changed the way you view life or changed the way you thought about yourself? How long since you have been impacted by a God-thought?

I'll tell you what happens when you get a God-thought. You scramble for a pen and immediately begin to write it down. When was the last time you turned on the light at night, got out of bed and began writing down a thought from God? When was the last time you pulled over to the side of the road to write down what God was saying into your heart as you were driving to work? When was the last time you heard a thought from God?

Vast thoughts

"How vast is the sum" of His thoughts. God isn't stingy with His thoughts. He doesn't give you a thought once a decade. He doesn't give you a thought once every five, ten or fifteen years. His thoughts are vast and innumerable. He has so many thoughts that you cannot even imagine how many are coming your way.

Defining thoughts

The Hebrew word for thought encompasses the idea of intentions, purposes, designs and dreams. It refers to the thoughts and purposes that fill a person's mind. When you think about the thoughts of God, put these five words to work:

- God's intentions for your life.
- God's purposes for your life.
- God's designs for your life.
- God's thoughts for your life.
- God's dreams for your life.

When you begin to feel the intentions of God for your life, when you begin to see His purposes and designs, to hear His thoughts and see His dreams, you begin to change. You begin to imagine life much different than it is right now. You begin to imagine a life lived as God sees it.

Receiving the thoughts of God

Many, O Lord my God, are Your wonderful works which You have done; and Your thoughts toward us cannot be recounted to You in order; if I would declare and speak of them, they are more than can be numbered. *(Psalm 40:5)*

God's thoughts are toward us. Toward means it is coming our way. It has the idea of throwing something into a container. We are the containers and God is throwing His thoughts into us.

Do you remember playing catch when you were a child? I played baseball when I was in school, so it's the sport I always wanted my kids to play. Boy or girl, my children had to have a baseball when they were little. At first I would roll it to them. As soon as they got big enough to stand up, I would bounce it to them. When they got bigger, I would throw it to them so they could catch it. It wasn't easy for them to learn. They would stand with their hands wide apart, waiting for it. "Put your hands together. Like this. Okay, now just catch it. I'll throw it right into your hands. You just catch it." But they would open their hands and let it fall between them, or they would fall down and the ball would bounce off their head. But I kept throwing it and they kept trying until they caught the ball every time I threw it.

The thoughts of God are coming your way today. He is pitching thoughts toward you. "Here they come, son. Here they come, daughter. Here's a thought. Get your hands ready. Put that faith mitt on. Get ready to catch it. I'm throwing some things your way and I want you to catch them. Are you ready?"

Waiting for God's thoughts

How can we be ready to catch God's thoughts? The Bible says that we must wait on the Lord, listen to His voice and be open to hear what He says. But so often we stand with our arms folded and a frown on our face, "Give it your best shot God. Nice pitch, but I just don't believe it. I'm not even going to try to catch it because the last time I did nothing happened. I've caught those thoughts before and they didn't change anything, so why try now. From now on I'm just going to stand here with my arms folded. If you want me to catch a thought, you have to bean me in the head with it. Then maybe I'll believe it."

Ask God to forgive you for an attitude of unbelief and a reluctance to receive His thoughts. Then put up your faith mitt and begin to wait on Him, begin to read the scriptures and listen to the Holy Spirit. His thoughts are toward you. He desires to speak His thoughts to you because His thoughts are unique, inspired, and awesome. They are powerful, far superior to our thoughts for our life. They can fill your whole being. They push out the darkness, push out the negativity, and push out the smallness of soul and the carnal. They push out the non-God thoughts from your life so that you have a new fire, a new passion, a new understanding of His will for you.

God desires to speak His thoughts to you

God has unique and specific thoughts that are designed just for you for a specific time and a specific purpose. You aren't receiving the after-thoughts that are leftover after God thought about somebody else. He doesn't have leftover thoughts from thinking about Billy Graham so He tosses them toward you. He has specific thoughts for your life. He has specific thoughts for this exact time and season that you are in.

God desires to reveal His innumerable, awesome thoughts toward us to encourage us and to inspire us to greatness. He wants us to hit the mark

He has set for us in life. When God sends thoughts towards us, they change our lives. They alter the way we live. They change our direction and make us more fruitful, and we begin to live like the overcomers He says we are.

God desires to communicate His thoughts directly to us concerning our immediate needs, our future questions about life and the decisions we need to make. We don't have to twist His arm to get Him to throw His thoughts our way. He desires to touch our lives. He cares about us as individuals and wants to speak directly to us.

He wants us to listen carefully and diligently to what He has to say. He wants us to wait patiently and passionately for His thoughts and words. He wants us to stand ready to hear. Live with a pencil in hand, always ready to write down what He says. I understand we can't go through life with a pencil in our hand at all times, but we can do that in our spirit. In our spirit, we can maintain an attitude of alertness, an ear that is always open and listening and a heart that is ready to receive and write into our lives what He speaks.

Discerning the thoughts aimed toward you

One of the problems we run into is that there many thoughts that are aimed toward us. Sometimes it's hard to discern which one is from God and where the other thoughts are from.

• *Thoughts from your own mind*

Because the carnal mind is enmity against God; for it is not subject to the law of God, nor indeed can be. (Romans 8:7)

There are thoughts in motion toward you from your own limited or carnal mind. They are thoughts that pull you down. They are thoughts that stir self-ishness in you and encourage you to act without integrity. They twist your perception of things and encourage you to wrongly use people or situations to get ahead in life. If a thought serves only yourself, it's probably not a God-thought. God doesn't speak selfishness into our lives. He doesn't want us to be selfish. *(Romans 7:14)*

• *Thoughts from your past*

For the weapons of our warfare are not carnal but mighty in God for pulling down strongholds, casting down arguments and every high thing that exalts itself against the knowledge of God, bringing every thought into captivity to the obedience of Christ, and

being ready to punish all disobedience when your obe-
dience is fulfilled. (2 Corinthians 10:4-6)

Secondly, there are thoughts that come towards you from your past. They can be assumptions that you have always lived with and never challenged. They can be negative thinking ruts that trap you so you can't even begin to hear what God says. Every time faith tries to raise its voice, the negative rut takes over and pushes it away. That negative rut says, "Don't start. You'll be disappointed. Don't try. It won't work. Don't believe in it. Don't reach for something better. Give up."

- *Thoughts from the enemy of your soul*

  But He answered and said, "It is written, 'Man shall not live by bread alone, but by every word that proceeds from the mouth of God.' " (Matthew 4:4)

Thirdly, there are the thoughts that come toward you from the enemy of your soul. Ephesians 6:12 says, "For we do not wrestle against flesh and blood, but against principalities, against powers, against the rulers of the darkness of this age, against spiritual hosts of wickedness in the heavenly places."

The devil is a liar. He will lie to you about yourself, about God, about the Bible, about prayer, about your life, about your past, about your future. He will lie about everything. He throws doubt and unbelief in and builds a lie.

Here are some of his most common lies. When you hear these, you need to immediately take up the shield of faith from Ephesians 6:16-17 and come against these lies with the truth of God's word.

- *You don't have a dream.*

    You do have a dream. If there is breath in your lungs, if you have a pulse in your wrist, then you have a dream and it isn't too late to see it fulfilled.

- *You don't need a dream.*

    You do need a dream. God never intended for you to have a purposeless life, lived only to please yourself. He has a dream for you. He has a God-thought for you. And that dream will happen.

- *Your dream will never succeed.*

    God said that His word will never come back to Him without accomplishing its purpose. Your dream will succeed, not because of you but because of God.

- *Your past has cancelled God's dream for you.*

    You made the wrong decision. You married the wrong person. You took the wrong job. You will never achieve what you thought you would do. You thought you would be a missionary, but look at you now. You thought you'd be a businessman, but you've gone bankrupt every time you tried. Give up. Your past has ruined you for what God has for you.

These are all lies! God is bigger than that. The past has not ruined you for God's purposes. That belittles God. It belittles His word. He is bigger than that!

• *You will be disappointed, so why start?*

Romans 5:5 says, "Now hope does not disappoint, because the love of God has been poured out in our hearts by the Holy Spirit who was given to us." God loves you. He will not promise you something and then take it back. Your hope, your faith, is not based on your ability to see it happen but on the faithfulness of the God who promised. Just before the previous verse, Paul says Abraham believed that he would not be disappointed. His faith was not in his own ability to see the promise fulfilled. He knew better than that! His faith was in the character and nature of God. Is God who He says He is? Then you can trust Him and know He will not disappoint you.

- *Your dream isn't important.*

Other people's dreams are important, but yours isn't. God doesn't care about politics. Why are you dreaming about changing anything in that world? You can't change politics. There is too much dirt and filth and corruption. Your dream is not that important. God's not that concerned with children or education or selling groceries. Whatever your dream is, it isn't important to God.

- *Your dream is too late.*

This is a lie that the enemy uses with many people. You started too late. It's too late for anything to happen. Faith felt called to the mission field when she was in her late teens but she didn't step foot on the field until she was 60. Wini dreamed of joining the Peace Corp when she was 24. She finally did, 39 years later at the age of 65. Evelyn had always dreamed of being a flight attendant, but worked her entire life as a bank vice-president. When she retired, she resurrected that dream and went to work for an airline, becoming a flight attendant at the ripe young age of 71. [2] And we can't forget Abraham and Sarah who became parents at 100 years of age. Too late for you? Why?

But the Lord said to Samuel, "Do not look at his appearance or at the height of his stature, because I have refused him. For the Lord does not see as man sees; for man looks at the outward appearance, but the Lord looks at the heart." *(1 Samuel 16:7)*

There are thoughts toward you from people who know you. They can be parents, friends or teachers who know you but they don't know what God has put in your heart. They may not have faith for God's dream for you. They don't know what God has spoken into your heart.

They are people like David's brother. David was bringing his brother's lunch to him on the front lines of the battle. He saw Goliath screaming and yelling, blaspheming God and David said, "What's with that uncircumcised Philistine over there?" The soldiers just shrugged. They were used to hearing Goliath taunting and didn't want to aggravate an angry bully who was twice their size.

But David was a giant-killer in the making. He was a man of God in the making. He had a heart that ran to the challenge. His brothers couldn't identify with that so they told him, "Go back and take care of your sheep. Go back, David. You're just a proud little sheep boy. You just came to see the battle. You don't understand what's going on here. Go back to the things you do know—your sheep."

They couldn't understand a giant-killing heart. They couldn't understand the heart of a boy who was becoming a king. Sometimes people will say things to you that are wrong, limited or critical. They want to shrink you to fit their world. Don't answer them back. Don't get angry at them. Just smile and say, "But God." Remember that phrase, but God. But God is in this, so it can work. But God said, so I can.

- *Thoughts from your world culture*

I beseech you therefore, brethren, by the mercies of God, that you present your bodies a living sacrifice, holy, acceptable to God, which is your reasonable service. And do not be conformed to this world, but be transformed by the renewing of your mind, that you may prove what is that good and acceptable and perfect will of God. *(Romans 12:1-2)*

The world's culture is negative and twisted. Those who see things from the perspective of our culture see things wrong. They say things wrong. They can't understand God's perspective. Romans 12:1-2 pleads with us to not allow the way the world thinks to put restrictions on how we think. We need to think as God thinks and to hear God's thoughts.

- *Thoughts from God*

"For I know the thoughts that I think toward you," says the Lord, " thoughts of peace, and not of evil, to give you an expected end." *(Jeremiah 29:11)*

Finally, there are thoughts toward you from God. These are true thoughts. They are reality far more than the world we live in is reality. God's thoughts will change your life. Meditate on these God-thoughts:

- God has rescued me from the dark power of Satan's rule and has brought me into His kingdom.
- God has cleansed me from all sin. I am pure and holy, whole and beautiful.
- God has forgiven me all of my sins and my past.
- God has my life written out in His book and He has plans for me.
- God has bought me with His blood. I am important, significant and special.
- God has destined me to be blessed, favored and fruitful.
- God is committed to changing me so I can live my dream.
- God has chosen me for great things.
- God has given me a dream and a hope for my future.

Imagine in agreement with God's will

A person who knows and walks with God imagines differently than someone who does not. The person who does not know God has no guidelines on his imagining. He can imagine anything he likes and go wherever he wants, good or bad. It is his life, his future and his decisions. He has no higher standard to line up with, no greater purpose.

For the believer, imagining is done within the context of Scripture and a God-thought. Imagining takes place through Christ in us. It is not just us imagining what we want. We are trying to imagine what God has in store for us, to see the dream He has already painted for our life. To imagine biblically, we must have a divine perspective on our life.

It is not about me using my wildest imagination and trying to make it happen. It is tapping into God's greater vision and His purpose for my life that causes me to sacrifice myself in order to make an impact on those around me. This is not about you thinking up anything you want and believing it will happen. It's not about you asking God for anything that your heart desires and expecting Him to give it to you. We must see this in the context of the Bible, in the context of the Kingdom of God.

Imagine in agreement with God's Word

Matthew 6:33 tells us to "Seek first the kingdom of God and His righteousness, and all these things shall be added to you." If you don't understand the Lordship of Christ over your life, if you don't have a kingdom of God mentality, then you will imagine the wrong things. You must first seek the kingdom of God, making Christ Lord over your life, bending your will to match His will, putting to death selfishness and carnality in your life, and seeking to serve the living God. If you do this, you will imagine in agreement with His will.

To know God's thoughts, you must know His word. You must get the Word of God into your life. If you want to have a great dream for your life, get into the Word of God. Read it, study it, memorize it, meditate on it. If you want to know God, consume the Bible. If you are not sure what you could or should do, start with the things that the Bible clearly says.

Start with the obvious things that it says to do. Consume the Word of God so that it fills your life, then your thinking will become aligned with the Bible. Your dreams and visions will become aligned with the Bible. From that written word will come the quickened word and the Holy Spirit will speak into your spirit the quickened or prophetic thoughts that God is speaking to you.

A Prayer of Alignment

Lord God, I align my life with Your word. I value your written word and live according to what You have said. I align my life with Your will, bending my will to yours. Your thoughts toward me are good thoughts and I place my life into Your hands, trusting Your thoughts for me and living my life in agreement with them.

Chapter 4

Imagine is a Holy Spirit Word

Matt Emmons had a dream—an Olympic gold medal. He had already earned one and was looking for his second. It was the final round of the 50-meter three-position rifle final and Matt was nervous. Leading by three points, he only needed to score an 8.0 on this shoot, getting near the bull's-eye to win. He focused on staying calm and carefully aimed at the target. He nailed it! Top score! An 8.1! Another gold medal to take home! But when the scores were posted he only came in eighth in the competition. He had made a great shot and a great score—at the wrong target. [1]

You can have a great dream. You can even hit it. You can accomplish great things in your life, but if you hit the wrong target it doesn't count. I don't want to shoot at someone else's target. I don't want to hit the bull's eye on a lesser goal. I want to hit the God-goal. I don't want to be a big achiever in the wrong arena; I want to achieve what God wants me to achieve.

Are you hitting the right target?

To the world it may look like you missed the target, but you scored a bull's-eye on God's target. Your achievement might look low to the world but high to God. You might turn down the promotion in your business because it means leaving your family for six months out of the year to travel. The promotion might be a bull's-eye but it could be on the wrong target. You can take the achiever route but lose things that might be greater: your marriage, your children, your health, or your local church involvement. You might lose spiritual ground to gain financial ground. Everyone else may applaud in amazement as you nail the bull's-eye, but God only sees the wrong target you are hitting. You can accomplish great things in life and at the end look back and say, "I wish I would have aimed higher because that target wasn't worth it." I want you to shoot the right target.

You cannot reach your goal without the Holy Spirit

Eye has not seen, nor ear heard, nor have entered into the heart of man the things which God has prepared for those who love Him. (1 Corinthians 2:9)

The Holy Spirit is your partner in shooting the target of life. He knows the will of God and will intercede so that you might adjust your life to meet the will of God. He is the one who adjusts your sights so you are aiming at the right goal. You are born of the Spirit. You need to be filled with the Spirit and walk in the Spirit. You need to hear and be empowered by the Spirit.

Who is preparing your future?

What has God prepared for you? God is a God of eternity and He sees the future just as clearly as He sees today. As He looks down on you today, He also sees who you are going to be tomorrow, next month, next year. With His foreknowledge (knowing in advance), God has already prepared the way for your life. He has pre-determined your boundary lines and prepared your future.

You can try to prepare your own future. You can allow your parents or your friends to prepare your future. They love you and they want a good future for you. You parents can be awesome and have good plans for your life. Your grandparents or friends or teachers or coaches can have ideas about your future. They may all be amazing people, but their perspective is limited in comparison to God's knowledge of your life.

The Holy Spirit knows what God's best is for your life. He knows the target for you to aim at and He will guide you to hit the mark. He may speak through your parents or friends. He will use your parents and teachers, but you must hear from God for yourself. 1 Corinthians 2:10 says that "God has revealed them (these things) to us through His Spirit. For the Spirit searches all things, yes, the deep things of God." Through the Holy Spirit we can know the things God has prepared for our future.

We are spirit beings

At creation God spoke and everything was created by His spoken word. He spoke and suddenly there was a huge sun where there had only been dark, empty space. He spoke and animals suddenly began to walk around on the earth and birds flew through the air and fish swam in the sea. Genesis 2:7 says that when God made man He didn't just speak, but He "breathed into his nostrils the breath of life; and man became a living being." He breathed His own breath into man. Nothing else has the breath of God. Only man. Into the very framework of His creation, He breathed into us the ability to reason, the capacity to understand and to be creative. He made us in His own image. We are spirit beings.

As unbelievers, our spirit was dead to God because of sin. When it came to spiritual things, we were blind, staring into the dark as we tried to understand God and find meaning to life. We could not hear the voice of God and could not relate to Him. Until a person's spirit is born again, it's dead and it can't hear God or relate to Him or understand the spiritual realm. Even if someone goes to church and has religious experiences and sings religious songs, unless the spirit has been born anew they cannot experience God.

When we are born anew, we can commune with God

After salvation, the Bible says that the eyes of my understanding are opened and I can see and understand. I become alive to God and can respond to Him. Maybe I can't hear clearly all the time, but I am growing in my ability to hear. I can learn to hear His voice more and to discern what He is saying to me. I have a new spirit that knows God and can commune with Him.

Do you know what your friend or spouse is thinking? Can you tell what the person next to you at work is thinking? The only person who knows what is going on inside a person's head is that person. It's the same way with God. 1 Corinthians 2:11-12 says, "For what man knows the things of a man except the spirit of the man which is in him? Even so no one knows the things of God except the Spirit of God. Now we have received, not the spirit of the world, but the Spirit who is from God, that we might know the things that have been freely given to us by God. When our spirit is born again and the Holy Spirit dwells in us, then He can help us to know the thoughts of God." *(Ephesians 2:1,5; 1 Corinthians 6:17-20; Proverbs 20:27; Romans 8;15-16)*

The three components of our born-again spirit

When our spirit is born anew, there are three parts to it that come to life: intuition, communion and conscience. These help us to begin to hear God's thoughts toward us.

- *Intuition*

  But immediately, when Jesus perceived in His spirit that they reasoned thus within themselves, He said to them, "Why do you reason about these things in your hearts?" (Mark 2:8)

Intuition is when the spirit in you senses the thoughts, feelings and desires of God. It comes directly from the Holy Spirit without reason or cause. It isn't from your mind, but from the very depths of your being. From deep inside, you begin to move with a God-thought and mold your life to be in agreement with what the Spirit is saying. Intuition is to know things by the revelation of the Holy Spirit, who enables you to lay hold of a particular truth by speaking the reality of it to your spirit. *(John 13:21; Acts 17:16; 1 John 2:26-27)*

• *Communion*

> *God is Spirit, and those who worship Him must worship in spirit and truth. (John 4:24)*

Communion is your ability to relate to and interact with God. It is the ability to receive revelation. God opens you up and pours into you something that does not come through human reasoning or the human mind. It comes by revelation of God directly into your spirit. Many times in the Gospels it says that Jesus felt deeply in His spirit. He was troubled in His spirit; He sighed in His spirit; He spoke from His spirit or discerned with His spirit. The Apostle Paul uses the same terminology. It is something spoken deep into your spirit because you have the ability to commune with God.

We communicate with the material world through the spoken word or through non-verbal communication with our body. We communicate with the spiritual world through the spirit. The Holy Spirit is the one who searches all things and knows the depths of God. He is the one who brings us into communication with God.

- *Conscience*

  *Pray for us; for we are confident that we have a good
  conscience , in all things desiring to live honorably.
  (Hebrews 13:18)*

Finally, we must have a clear conscience before God. The conscience is where God expresses His holiness in reproving sin and approving what is right. It speaks to us before we sin, not just afterward. It is the knowledge or feeling of right or wrong. It is the part of a person that decides if something is sin or not sin, if we should do it or not do it. It is the compulsion to do right that pressures us from within before we take action. It is meant to be an inner guide that approves or disapproves of our decisions and actions. Even though you might reason about what you want to do in life or what you want to dream about, the Holy Spirit may speak through your conscience and say, "That's not right for you. It might be right for him or her, but not for you."

If your conscience is unclean or twisted or seared, you'll have a hard time hearing the voice of God or moving into the ways of God. Your conscience becomes your prompter. It warns you of a wrong decision you are making before you make it. Have you ever had this gnawing feeling in the pit of your stomach that something isn't right? You can't put your finger on it, but something is wrong. The

Holy Spirit is welling up inside of you and saying, "That's a wrong step for you. That will cost you in the long run. Don't go that way."

Your conscience confirms or restrains your decisions

Your conscience can be a restraint that comes into your spirit. It could be in a relationship. You've just started getting to know this person and he or she looks like the person you would want to develop a relationship with. The person is a good Christian, goes to church, loves God, has the same interests as you. It all looks good. Then something inside you says, "Wait. This isn't right." And your response is, "I rebuke you, devil! How can this be wrong? This is the perfect person!" But something inside you that is beyond reasoning prompts you that this is the wrong target. God has a different target for you. So you back up and wait for the right one. (Acts 24:16; Romans 2:15; 2 Corinthians 1:12; 1 Timothy 1:5; 2 Timothy 4:2)

This can apply to any arena of life. You need a clear conscience that prompts you, approves or disapproves, confirms or restrains. It could be in the area of your career. You went to seven years of school, have a great job and now are being offered a promotion that pays six figures a year. Everything says go, but inside God says, "No, don't go there. I want you to go to Uganda to help in an orphanage for a year."

"What? This is a once in a lifetime career opportunity! I need to make this money so I can buy a house and get married." You wrestle with it, pray about it and the only time you get peace is when you say yes to the inner voice of the Holy Spirit. You go to Uganda or South Africa or wherever He is calling you. Your coworkers look at you like you lost your mind. Your friends think you're crazy. But all you can say is, "This is what God has told me to do." So you go work in the orphanage and surprise, surprise. There's this woman who wrestled with the same decision but listened to God and came to work in that country as well. You cross paths, get to know each other, and God whispers into your ear, "She's better than a promotion, isn't she?"

If you had to choose between a promotion or marrying the woman you love, would you choose the promotion? Of course not! But you don't know that's what you're choosing when the Holy Spirit is speaking to you. You can only see the decision in front of you, not the long-term result of it.

God sees the long-term.

Fourteen years ago I made a decision that did not make any sense to me, my wife, my church leadership or my future. I had planted a church in Eugene, Oregon, and my heart was there. I was staying there the rest of my life. Then one day God came in and said, "Frank, I want to talk to you about your future."

"Sure, God. What do you want to tell me?"

"Go serve another man's vision."

I was driving down the road in my car and talking out loud. "What are you talking about? What do you mean serve another man's vision? I have a vision. I'm a visionary in case you haven't noticed. I have a personal vision. I don't need someone else's vision. And I have a successful church. I don't need to go serve at someone else's church."

God replied to me, "Your days here are numbered. You're on assignment. You're leaving."

My whole life fell apart. It was the hardest decision I had ever made as an adult. But I knew this was God. I didn't know the end of it. I just knew this is God. He made it abundantly clear. At the time, all I saw was what I was leaving. I couldn't see the future fourteen years down the road. All I could see was that day and the difficulty of leaving. But God knew the future of that decision and I trusted Him with my future, a future of hope and destiny.

God's thoughts aren't always our thoughts. His destiny for our lives isn't always what we think our destiny is. He may set a target in front of us but we're too busy looking around at other people's targets to focus on what He has set in front of us.

Sometimes His destiny isn't comfortable for us. His target isn't easy for us to consider. God says, "Seek first My kingdom." Fulfillment comes when we seek His will first, not ours. As you set your heart to seek His kingdom and His righteousness, as you set your will to be in agreement with His will, as you set your spirit to hear and respond to His voice, you will find a destiny of great fulfillment and satisfaction.

Think about the following seven statements about imagining. Read through the scriptures and pray these into your life.

- *Imagining is to receive the dreams God has for you. (1 Corinthians 2:9)*

  At Gibeon the Lord appeared to Solomon in a dream by night; and God said, "Ask! What shall I give you?" (1 Kings 3:5)

Stop and ask God, "What dreams do you have for me? What do you want for my life?" Maybe you have some dreams; lay them before God and ask if these are His dreams or yours, His thoughts or yours. Be willing to give up your dreams and your thoughts and take up His dreams and His thoughts. For His are far greater than ours.

- *Imagining is to see the future without limitations or restrictions. (Genesis 12:1-3)*

  For I know the thoughts that I think toward you, says the Lord, thoughts of peace and not of evil, to give you a future and a hope. (Jeremiah 29:11)

God has a future for you that no one else has ever had. He has a future for you that will necessitate miracles, a future that is somewhere between highly unlikely to nearly impossible. It is a future that will impact generations to come. There is no proof that this future will ever be reality, but you can believe it and by faith walk into it.

- *Imagining is the Holy Spirit opening our hearts and revealing His secrets. (Matthew 6:4-6; Romans 2:16; 1 Corinthians 14:25)*

  But God has revealed them to us through His Spirit. For the Spirit searches all things, yes, the deep things of God. (1 Corinthians 2:10)

There are things inside you that even you are not aware of, things the Holy Spirit has placed within you. There are hidden treasures and dreams that the Holy Spirit is going to begin to dig out and bring to the surface in your life.

- *Imagining is to believe what was impossible in the past is now possible. (Mark 10:27; 17:20)*

  Jesus said to him, 'If you can believe, all things are possible to him who believes. (Mark 9:23)

If you move in faith and with God and His will, what is possible? Don't judge your future based on the past. God is a God of new beginnings. You can start new today and leave the failures and frustrations from yesterday in order to run into a great future in God.

- *Imagining is to lift the lid of your mind and resist old assumptions. (Colossians 3:1-2)*

  Do not remember the former things, nor consider the things of old. Behold, I will do a new thing, now it shall spring forth; shall you not know it? I will even make a road in the wilderness and rivers in the desert. (Isaiah 43:18-19)

Get rid of old thinking patterns. Get out of the old ruts of how you think about yourself and your future. Don't make decisions based on the old assumptions from the past. Take the lid off! Think God's thoughts!

- *Imagining is to let go of lesser ambitions. (Joshua 8:18; Philippians 3:13)*

  Isaiah 54:2-3 "Enlarge the place of your tent, and let them stretch out the curtains of your dwellings; Do not spare; Lengthen your cords, and strengthen your stakes. For you shall expand to the right and to the left, and your descendants will inherit the nations, and make the desolate cities inhabited."

Isaiah 54 says to "enlarge your tent." We set up our tent, stretching it tight, pounding down the tent pegs and then step back and say, "Okay God, here's the tent. Fill it up." But God says, "Nope. It's too small. Get longer cords, get bigger stakes. Stretch the cords out further and pound the stakes down deeper. You're willing to settle for one child but I have nations for you. You are willing to settle for one small piece of ground but I have a whole world needing to be reached."

- *Imagining is to make a faith declaration of what you see. (Job 22:28; Romans 4:17)*

  Psalms 40:10 "I have not hidden Your righteousness within my heart; I have declared Your faithfulness and Your salvation; I have not concealed Your loving kindness and Your truth from the great assembly."

Proverbs 18:21 states, "Death and life are in the power of the tongue." Your words have power. They have the power to kill a dream or give life to a dream. Begin to speak what God has said. God told Abram he would have children so he changed his name to Abraham, "father of a multitude." For a whole year

Abraham went around calling himself the father of a multitude while he was childless. In faith he declared every day the reality of something he could not see.

It's not enough to get the thought of God. You must write it down and begin to confess it as true. If you have lesser goals, let them go and begin to confess God's higher goal for your life. Put the words in front of you and pray them daily and let the Holy Spirit make them real in your life.

Prayer of Confession

> *Father, right now I confess any sin that is in my life that I might live with a clear conscience before you. I will hide no unconfessed sin in my life because I want to live hearing Your voice and walking in obedience to Your voice. I lay aside all my own ambitions and desires and seek only Your will and Your dreams for my life. I set aside the things I have held onto that I might grasp hold of what You want to give me.*

Chapter 5

Imagine is a Vision Word

Choose the imperishable. See the invisible. Do the impossible. In order to choose the imperishable things of God, we must see with the eye of faith, looking at the invisible and seeing in the spirit God's dream for our life. We need to listen to His voice and trade our plan for our lives for God's plan for our lives and pursue that with everything in us.

Imagine is a vision word. It is a word that sees into the future and into the invisible realm. It is a faith word, reaching into the unknown. It is the promise of what is to come, the title deed of what is yours but does not yet exist. But you must reach for it.

Why do some people never have a dream for their life?

"The greatest tragedy in life is people who have sight, but no vision." These words were spoken by

Helen Keller, blind from childhood. Although she was blind and deaf and could not speak, she made a profound impact on her world and was named by Time magazine as one of the 100 most important people of the century.

There are many people who have seeing eyes, but not a seeing heart. If you don't have heart vision, you will grope and stumble through life. You will never fulfill what God has for you. Vision is the act or power of seeing with the eyes of the heart, causing anticipation and expectation as your eyes are fixed on the future mark or goal.

We are made in the image of God. That means we are to be people who live purposefully. To do that, we must have an encounter with God. Our hearts have to see with the eyes of the Holy Spirit what God has for our lives.

What marks your life?

What is the most important thing in your life? What makes you get up in the morning? What makes you the happiest person on earth? What makes you unique? What is your passion? What is the first thing that comes into your mind when I say Bill Gates or Mother Teresa? These are people who had a vision and a passion that consumed their lives. That vision was so strong it marked their identity forever.

You will never think of Muhammad Ali and think of baseball or car racing. His passion marked who you perceive him to be. What is your passion? What marks your life?

Other people can look at you and wonder why you are so happy when you are living your passion. What is it about working with kids that makes you so excited? Why do you get so passionate about teaching ESL? How can you enjoy working as a banker? When you have a vision for God's will for your life, that vision will propel you into a future of delight and fulfillment.

The power of accepting responsibility

Many people live in the past. It is safe and predictable. Even if the past was bad, at least you were familiar with it. You don't know what the potential bad is in the future, so you decide to stay in the bad that you do know instead of risk the bad you don't know.

Identical twin brothers were raised together in the same family, under the same roof, yet their lives were worlds apart. One was an alcoholic who lived a visionless life. The other one never touched alcohol and lived a strong purposeful life. They both were asked a simple question, "Why are you the way you are?" Their answers were the same yet with a different result. They both said, "I was raised by an alcoholic father, so how could I be anything else?" But the alcoholic went on to say it was the only example he had to follow so he followed it; he had no other choice in life. His twin acknowledged he was raised by an alcoholic father but his father had given him an example of what he did not want to be.

Vision is greater than circumstances

In our culture we blameshift for everything. It's because of the way we grew up; it's because of where we live. We blame the politicians, the President, the family tree, our father, our mother, our teachers, and our living environment. We blame everybody and everything. We blame McDonalds because we don't have the self-discipline to not overeat and we blame the kid sitting next to us in school because he didn't cover his paper so we couldn't cheat.

It's not anyone else's responsibility. It's yours. You must take responsibility for your dream. If you blameshift, you will never get anywhere. Twenty years from now you will be in the same place you are now if you believe it's always someone else's fault. Do you want to have a future? Then take responsibility for your decisions.

Vision determines your future

For many years I have carried a poem in my wallet. When I was a teenager I was pouring out my heart to my pastor's wife as she was cleaning her kitchen. As she scrubbed dishes, I talked of my life and how I didn't have a clear vision. I was in junior college studying business. Should I keep doing that? Should I stop and go to Bible school or should I learn a trade?

In the middle of my conversation, Rozella grabbed a towel, dried her hands and picked up a pen and a little card. Sitting down at the table next to me, she put one arm around my shoulders and wrote this poem down.

"Great it is to believe the dream
As we stand in youth by the starry stream;
But a greater thing is to fight life through
And say at the end, the dream is true!"

"Frank, if you could go to the end of your life, what would you want to end with?" As a 19-year-old, I was captured by her question. "Just imagine your 70th birthday. Looking back to when you were 20, would you have a clear enough dream that you could say, 'My dream is true. I lived for that dream and look what has happened!'?"

> **"The greatest tragedy in life is people who have sight, but no vision."**
>
> —*Helen Keller*

Imagine

When you reflect back on your life, will you look back with regrets and tears because of what did not happen? Your dream should carry you through life and you should be able to say at the end, "What a journey! What a way to live! If I had it to do over again, I'd do it the same."

Vision changes the way you live

As you look ahead at your life, think about these questions that you would ask yourself at the end. What did my life add up to? What did I live for? Did it really matter? Who will remember me and what will they say? What will I leave behind that is greater than me? Now use those answers to change the way you are living now.

In Acts 26:19, Paul tells King Agrippa, "I was not disobedient to the heavenly vision." You have a vision that God wants to give you. There is a supernatural encounter God wants to have with you. There is something He wants to drop into your heart that you might pursue it. He wants you to live with purpose.

The Bible has a lot to say about people who are wanderers and vagabonds in life. They can't see the vision, can't make up their mind what to do. Their life is unfruitful. When they get to heaven, they are saved but there is nothing fruitful in their lives except salvation. They have no crowns to lay at Jesus' feet. I don't want you to be that kind of person. I want you to be a person with a heavenly vision who lives life with purpose and passion.

Vision requires perseverance

Since we are surrounded by so great a cloud of witnesses, let us lay aside every weight and the sin which so easily ensnares us, and let us run with endurance the race that is set before us. (Hebrews 12:1)

William Carey was captured by a vision. He was convinced that the people of the world needed Christ and that Christ wanted him to go tell them about Him. For 41 years he lived in India, fulfilling that vision. The first seven of those years he saw no fruit from his vision. No one got saved, his wife's health deteriorated, others did not understand or fully support his vision. But at the end of his life, he could look back and see many people saved, the Bible translated and printed into forty of the Indian dialects, a Bible college built and more missionaries coming to India and to other countries around the world. When asked what the secret was to the success of the vision, he very simply replied, "I can plod."

Living with vision is not a sprint, but a marathon. It isn't a quick dash for the goal, but a lifestyle of moving forward with perseverance. Hebrews says we are to "run with endurance." It is the picture of standing strong and holding up under pressure. Built into this concept is the idea of patience and courageous resistance in the face of adversity, of standing persistently in the face of opposition. We are to pursue the vision with patient endurance, with an unswerving willingness to await events rather than to try to force them. We are to stand our ground and to be willing to plod patiently without giving in to discouragement. Endurance is the "brave patience which lets nothing adverse force it to give up." [1]

Vision isn't accomplished overnight. It takes perseverance. Albert Einstein, considered one of the greatest geniuses of the 20th century, said, "I think and think for months and years. Ninety-nine times the conclusion is false, but the hundredth time I am right." After years of research, Louis Pasteur created the rabies vaccine, saving thousands of lives. He said, "Let me tell you the secret that has led me to my goal. My strength lies solely in my tenacity."

Don't give up! Pursue the vision with a patient reliance on God. Keep your eyes fixed on Him regardless of the discouragements and distractions that come against you.

Threats to perseverance

Staying the course isn't easy. We mustgrab hold of the vision and hold it in a death grip, determined to pursue wholeheartedly the purposes of God. We muststand with our hands clenched tight around the promises of God. If someone comes up and grabs one of our fingers and begins to pry it off the promise, that's okay. We still have nine fingers latched onto the promise so we're okay—until another situation arises that pries the next finger off and then another and another.

Hebrews 12 reveals threats to perseverance—things that try to pry our hands off the promises of God:

- *The threat of unconquered, insignificant sins*

  Let us lay aside every weight, and the sin which so easily ensnares us... (Hebrews 12:1)

The J.B. Phillips translation of Hebrews 12:1 reads, "Let us strip off everything that hinders us, as well as the sin which drags our feet." When the ancient Greeks ran in a race, they ran naked so there was nothing to encumber them, nothing to hold them back or get in their way. We need to lay aside everything that would hinder us from fulfilling the purposes of God. Sometimes those are sins that are easy for us to fall into because of our temperament or weaknesses or environment. Sometimes they are habits which provide open doorways to temptation. Sometimes the encumbrances are not necessarily sin but are habits or lifestyles that hinder us from putting our best into pursuing the vision.

- *The threat of undefined goals and purposes*

  Let us run with endurance the race that is set before us. (Hebrews 12:1)

Just like Matt Emmons, we can hit the mark but lose because we hit the wrong target. We must see clearly the goal ahead of us and we must be disciplined to reach that goal. Develop life disciplines that will enable you to run with perseverance. Develop good time management skills. Write out your vision statement and keep it in front of you so you don't get sidetracked by good but lesser goals.

- *The threat of deadly distractions*

  Our eyes fixed on Jesus, the source and the goal of our faith. (Hebrews 12:2 [Phillips])

At the Boston Marathon you can stand on the sidelines and watch the runners going by. As the lead runner goes by, you notice that he is casually waving at friends and onlookers and admiring the scenery, looking at the great architecture on some of the old buildings that he is passing. Not a chance!

He is running with his eyes fixed on the road ahead of him. He is looking away from everything else and can only see one thing—the goal ahead. We must allow nothing to turn us aside from the goals and vision that God has given us. Like Paul we must "press toward the goal for the prize of the upward call of God in Christ Jesus." *(Philippians 3:14)*

- *The threat of losing motivation*

  Looking unto Jesus, the author and finisher of our faith, who for the joy that was set before Him endured the cross, despising the shame, and has sat down at the right hand of the throne of God. (Hebrews 12:2)

Three men were working side by side in the hot sun. A man walking by asked them, "What are you doing?" The first worker replied, "Laying bricks." The second, "Building a wall." The third worker energetically replied, "I am raising a great cathedral." At 3:00 in the afternoon when the sun is at its peak, the wall ahead looks unending and weariness is setting in, which worker is going to be able to keep going? The one with vision.

When you begin to get discouraged and tired, remember the vision. Pull out that piece of paper and read it again. Remind yourself of God's promises. Remember why you began this race, refocus on the goal that lies ahead and renew your faith in the God who called you to do this. The God who called you to the vision is the one who will make sure the work is completed. You just have to keep running.

- *The threat of becoming weary*

  in order that you may not grow tired by relaxing in your souls. (Hebrews 12:3 [Lenski])

Aristotle used this word to refer to runners who make it to the end but then relax and collapse when they pass the finishing post. It is the gradual letting down of effort, the gradual slowing down. It is the relaxing of moral virtue, strength and soul disciplines after accomplishing the goal.

One of the most dangerous times is after great victories. Gideon was used by God to win a great battle, yet afterwards he relaxed his inner strength and led the people into idol worship. Solomon had a goal of building a great temple for the people to worship God. After it was completed, he relaxed and ended with the lament that "everything is vanity, useless and meaningless."

Keep up your guard. Never relax in your soul. Yes, you do need to take time for physical and mental relaxation but never for spiritual relaxation.

- *The threat of wrong focus*

  You have not yet resisted to bloodshed, striving against sin. (Hebrews 12:4)

Don't focus on your hardships or they will become greater than they really are. The more you look at your problems, the bigger they get. Don't let self-pity set in. Don't focus on the failure of the past, criticism from other people, or unwise decisions you have made. Don't be like the spies that Moses sent into the land who only saw the giants and not the bigness of their God. It is easy to get lost in a multitude of small problems and lose sight of the true goal. *(Romans 8:18; 2 Corinthians 4:17)*

- *The threat of reacting against God-sent correction*

  My son, do not despise the chastening of the Lord, nor be discouraged when you are rebuked by Him; for whom the Lord loves He chastens, and scourges every son whom He receives. (Hebrews 12:5-6)

God does not discipline us aimlessly but with a definite end in view. He wants to produce something good in your life. He disciplines from the heart of a father's love. Trust His discipline. It may not come through the channel you approve of, in the time you think it should or in the manner you desire. Even if God uses someone you don't like who says things you disagree with, hear the voice of the Spirit speaking into your inner man and respond to God in the situation.

- *The threat of discouragement*

  Therefore strengthen the hands which hang down, and the feeble knees, and make straight paths for your feet, so that what is lame may not be dislocated, but rather be healed. (Hebrews 12:12-13)

The Hebrews were allowing themselves to become disheartened. Discouragement was paralyzing them so they were told to brace themselves, straighten up and get ready to move forward.

Discouragement is not limited to the weak in faith or new believers. Elijah was a mighty prophet who had seen miracles in his ministry but he went and hid in the desert, moping and complaining to God that he was all alone and wanted to die *(1 Kings 19:14-18)*. Peter had walked with Jesus and knew Him well but he gave up and went fishing *(John 21:3)*.

Discouragement can come after great times of victory and rejoicing when God has delivered on His promise. Then the emotions of the victory wear off and weariness sets in, quickly followed by discouragement.

Discouragement can come after times of failure when we have failed in reaching a goal, hit the wrong goal or fallen into sin. Discouragement can be mild, a weight on your shoulders that makes it hard to lift your head up to see God. It can be strong, pushing you down so you find it difficult to lift your feet and keep moving. Or it can be disabling, leveling you flat on your face so you can see nothing but the failure in front of you.

We need strength to stand in the face of discouragement. This is the same word used by Luke in chapter 13 as he recounts the story of the woman who had been sick for 18 years. The disease had bent her over into a permanent stooped position, her face always toward the ground. When Jesus saw her, he laid hands on her and she was "made straight," standing strong and upright (Luke 13:13).

When discouragement has bent you to the ground, when it has undermined your foundation and leveled your vision, God will bring restoration and strength.

- *The threat of bitterness that weakens*

   Looking carefully lest anyone fall short of the grace of God; lest any root of bitterness springing up cause trouble, and by this many become defiled; lest there be any fornicator or profane person like Esau, who for one morsel of food sold his birthright. For you know that afterward, when he wanted to inherit the blessing, he was rejected, for he found no place for repentance, though he sought it diligently with tears. (Hebrews 12:15-17)

Imagine

Bitterness is a deep feeling of strong resentment towards someone or something. If you allow a small seed of bitterness to take root in your life, it will grow and affect the fruit that comes from your life. You cannot secretly foster feelings of resentment or jealousy towards one person and think it will not hurt you. Bitterness never remains small; it begins to contaminate other areas of your life and the fruit of your life takes on the same bitter taste.

Esau began with a small root of resentment and jealousy towards his brother. Jacob was his mother's favorite and got most of her attention. Esau's bitterness grew until the pressure of it allowed him to lose sight of the vision and give up his birthright, his most precious possession, for something that was insignificant and valueless.

Examples of Perseverance

In stark contrast to Esau, the Bible gives us examples of men who stood strong in the face of pressure and held onto the vision and purposes of God. These are men who made a commitment to the goal in times of pressure, who stood their ground and refused to give in to attacks, discouragement, misunderstandings or persecution. They set aside any privileges that would weaken their strength to stand.

- *David: Strengthened himself in God*

> *But David strengthened himself in the Lord his God.*
> *(1 Samuel 30:6)*

For 12 years David ran from Saul. He lived in caves and huts, always on guard, packing up and leaving whenever Saul came too close. He had finally found a safe place and settled down with his wives and family and then the enemy came in and took everything from him. He lost it all, his home, his family, and his wives. Just when he was at his lowest, his faithful followers joined in with their words of encouragement: "Look what David has done to us. Let's stone him!" Everybody was against him, everything was gone. Now what?

"David strengthened himself in the Lord his God." He didn't repeat to himself all the problems and go over them again and again in his mind. He fixed his gaze on God. He set his heart on the goal. He refused to allow distractions and discouragement to take root in his spirit. He declared, "This is my God. I will seek Him and do all His will."

- *Shammah: Stationed himself*

> *And after him was Shammah the son of Agee the Hararite. The Philistines had gathered together into a troop where there was a piece of ground full of lentils. So the people fled from the Philistines. But he stationed him-*

self in the middle of the field, defended it, and killed the Philistines. So the Lord brought about a great victory. (2 Samuel 23:11-12)

The Philistines were attacking and the Israelites ran. They saw the Philistine army coming and they turned tail and took off as fast as they could go. As they ran, someone asked, "Where's Shammah?" "I don't know. He was right behind me. Has anyone seen him?" Looking back over their shoulders, they saw him, a lone man standing in the face of a troop of enemy soldiers. "Shammah! You're crazy! Run!"

But Shammah "stationed himself in the middle of the field." He planted his feet firm in the ground he had been given and said, "This is my field. These are my lentils. I'm not moving." He made a stand in the face of overwhelming odds and won the victory.

- *Paul: Fought to the finish*

2 Timothy 4:7 "I have fought the good fight, I have finished the race, I have kept the faith."

Here's the latest best-seller on the life of Paul: Chapter 1, "Shipwrecked"; Chapter 2, "Beating"; Chapter 3, "Backstabbing Friends"; Chapter 4, "Disloyal Churches"; Chapter 5, "More Beatings." Look carefully. The one chapter you won't find is "Giving up." Paul didn't have a giving-up spirit. He never quit. He got to the end of his life, the end of his book, and he could declare, "I have fought the good fight. I have finished the race. I have kept the faith." That doesn't mean it was easy. He was discouraged at times, didn't know which way to go at times but he never gave up, never gave in, never quit (*2 Corinthians 4:8*).

Persevere in the vision. Follow the examples of these three men. When discouragement sets in, stand under the pressure and declare:

> *I will set my heart to seek God.*
> *I will stand in the midst of battle.*
> *I will fight to the finish.*

Six Types of Vision People

There are six types of vision people. As you read these, pray about them and ask yourself, "What type of vision person am I?"

- *People with no vision*

> *Where there is no revelation, the people cast off restraint; but happy is he who keeps the law. (Proverbs 29:18)*

These are people who walk aimlessly, making poor decisions and are unfruitful. At the end of their lives they look back and say, "I don't know what happened. Life just took me by storm and was here and gone. If I had it to do over again, I'd do it a lot differently." These are the people who lived life without ever stopping and asking God, "What is your vision?"

- *People with little vision*

  And the apostles said to the Lord, 'Increase our faith.' So the Lord said, 'If you have faith as a mustard seed, you can say to this mulberry tree, "Be pulled up by the roots and be planted in the sea," and it would obey you.' (Luke 17:5-6)

These are people with a small mind and a small faith for their future. They have some vision, but it's limited. They have limited vision because they have never stopped to apprehend the greatness of God. They have never talked to themselves about the goodness of God. They've never taken the faith scriptures of the Bible and applied them to their own lives. They need to start lifting their vision outside of themselves, outside of their own limitations and begin stretching their life to make room for God's vision for them.

Henry Ford said, "I'm looking for a lot of men with an infinite capacity for not knowing what can't be done." Allow the Holy Spirit to take the limits off your life and expand your capacity for doing anything that God asks you to do.

- *People with a confused vision*

> *For let not that man suppose that he will receive any-thing from the Lord; he is a double-minded man, un-stable in all his ways. (James 1:7-8)*

A confused vision is one that comes from a double-minded person. They go a little way down the road to one vision and then they switch to another track and pursue a different vision. Then another path crosses theirs and they jump onto that one and follow that vision. They can't decide which path is right, which vision they should pursue and whose counsel they should follow. They talk to a dozen different people and get two dozen different ideas. Their confusion immobilizes them.

There are people like this in their teens and people in their sixties and seventies. Age doesn't determine lack of or clarity of vision. They are always vacillating and wondering what to do. They are double-minded. That means they have two souls in them, two mindsets, two sets of emotion. They go back and forth, never decided what to do and never accomplishing anything. When delays happen, they get discouraged and question the vision.

You have to get rid of confusion. Get rid of double-mindedness. Find a secure place in God where you say, "This is what I'm supposed to do" and do it. If you're called to the marketplace, get into it and put your whole heart there. If you're called to medicine, get your degree now and get into med school. You can't afford to play around and try different things before pursuing the will of God.

One of the concerns I have is young people who think they can find the will of God when they get older. They drift through high school and then take a couple of years off after they graduate to "find themselves." They want to travel or work a mediocre job while they try to decide what the will of God is for their lives. Inaction leads to further inaction. The laws of physics say that a body in motion stays in motion and a body at rest stays at rest. The same law applies to our lives. If you put your vision to rest and go have fun, the vision will stay at rest and never go anywhere. If you want to be successful at fulfilling the will of God for your life, start young and don't waver. *(Psalm 119:113; 1 Corinthians 14:33)*

• *People with a vague vision*

Now the boy Samuel ministered to the Lord before Eli. And the word of the Lord was rare in those days; there was no widespread revelation. And it came to pass at that time, while Eli was lying down in his place, and when his eyes had begun to grow so dim that he could not see... (1 Samuel 3:1-2)

"People with God's vision have a spiritual desire to fulfill God's plan and purpose and are actively making decisions in alignment with that goal. This is the vision that brings joy and contentment to your life, the vision that declares, 'This is what I was born for.'"

These are people who live life in a fog. They have a little bit of vision but can't see clearly. When you drive down the interstate highway on a clear day, you can do 55 miles an hour but when it gets foggy you have to slow down. Why? Because you can't see clearly and may hit someone.

I don't know about you but I hate driving in the fog. I'm an impatient person and I don't like anything that makes me slow down. I just want to get out of the fog and out onto a clear road so I can hit the gas and go.

Come out of the fog in your life. Get a clear vision and go for God. Go ahead and break the speed limit—spiritually—but go wholeheartedly, all-out for God.

- *People with someone else's vision*

You might be living your parent's vision or your teacher's vision or a friend's vision. Perhaps someone told you that you have a talent in a certain area so you're going that direction. Maybe you took a personality test and it said you would be great at a certain career, but there is no passion in you for that.

You can fit in many places but don't have a passion for them. You can have many skills but no passion for that area of service. Your friends can push you a certain direction. Your teachers and family can push you a certain direction. But unless that vision is burned into your heart, you are living someone else's vision.

This doesn't mean you don't listen to counsel. God gave you your parents and teachers and pastors to be guides in your life and to bring balance and wisdom to your decisions. So get counsel. Listen to your parents. Listen to your teachers. But you must always hear the voice of God for yourself and not rely on them to hear for you.

• *People with God's vision*

Finally, there is the vision that comes from God. It is your bull's-eye, the target that God wants you to hit. The vision God has for your life. People with God's vision have a spiritual desire to fulfill God's plan and purpose and they are actively making decisions in alignment with that goal. This is the vision that brings joy and contentment to your life, the vision that declares, "This is what I was born for!"

As you match up your life and passions with the heart and will of God, you begin putting your talents to work for His purposes. This fills you with a motivation and passion because you are now tapping into the power of His dream for your life.

A Prayer for Passion

Lord God, help me to see the invisible, to see Your will and Your vision for my life. I don't want to be distracted by a lesser vision or by someone else's vision. I want to set my eyes clearly on you and to pursue with everything in me the call You have placed in my heart. Help me to choose the imperishable, to choose Your will above my own and to choose Your best for my life instead of my own or someone else's idea of what is good. Help me to do the impossible. As I persevere in my pursuit of the vision, accomplish the impossible through my life of obedience.

Chapter 6

Imagine is a Miracle Word

God-dream requires God-miracles. To imagine is to enter the world of miracles. In order to full the great vision that God has for your life, you must enter the world of our miracle-working God. If you try to do it all on your own, with your limited strength, you will not be able to accomplish all He wants. Without the supernatural intervention of God, you will not fulfill the God-dream that God has for your life. You need to step into the realm of miracles.

A God-sized dream takes God-sized miracles. If it's your dream, you don't need a miracle. If it is your future, you can probably make it happen. But if it's a God-future, you need divine resources, divine wisdom and divine strength. Through these you can produce far more in God than what the natural man can produce. If you only need your strength, abilities, wisdom and talents to make something happen, you're probably living out a dream that is a good dream but not a God-dream.

God wants to get you out of your comfort zone, out of the zone of your ease and abilities and into the zone of dependence on Him. Reach out and receive the miracles you need to fulfill God's dream for your life.

The definition of miracle

The word miracle can be defined as living beyond human or natural powers. It is moving into the supernatural, living above and beyond, superseding the limitations placed upon you by life, others or the devil. It is living beyond your own assumption of what is possible. A miracle is God's power invading your life in order to accomplish His purposes. It is a continuous work of God that will not be stopped or limited.

Divine sovereignty and human responsibility

There are two sides to balance as you move toward a dream—divine sovereignty and human responsibility. Divine sovereignty is God's power. He knows everything and can do anything. He is Lord of all. He opens doors and closes doors. He is God.

The other side is human responsibility. You are not sovereign. You have limitations. You don't know everything or see everything, but you do have a responsibility to respond to the dream and to work with God. Human responsibility means that you take steps and actions to make the dream that God has put in your heart come to pass. God may open the door or close the door, but you have to knock on it. He will guide your feet but you have to move them and walk. You have to begin to move. You have to move your life in the direction that God is directing and then He will open the doors.

Some people are so into the sovereignty of God that they just sit back and let God do everything. Just imagine: Susie is single and believes that God wants her to marry a doctor so they can do short-term medical missions together. So she sits on her couch, eats bonbons and watches medical shows on television as she waits for God to bring a doctor to her door.

Human responsibility says if you want to marry a doctor, get off your couch. Stop working at a grocery store and go work in a hospital where the doctors work. Find out where the doctors are and go there. If you are there, God can open a doctor's eyes to see you. Don't expect God to supernaturally speak to a doctor in a dream and say, "Go to this house on this street and knock on the door and your future wife will be waiting for you."

If you want to be a businessman, go to business school and begin to learn about business management and accounting and marketing. If you can't balance your own budget, you can't run a business. Go hang around successful business people and learn from them. Don't go hang out with college drop-outs to learn about business principles. You have to put yourself in a place to see the dream fulfilled. God will open the doors but you have to be standing in front of the door to walk through.

Joash stopped short

In 2 Kings 3:18-19, Joash, the king of Israel, is being attacked by the king of Syria. Elisha, the prophet of God, says to him, "Take these arrows and shoot the ground with them." In those days, shooting an arrow toward an enemy's country signified declaring war on that enemy. So Joash shoots one arrow into the ground, then a second and a third.

The prophet angrily tells him, "Why did you do that? Why did you stop? Why were you half-hearted in declaring war on the enemy? You should have shot all those arrows at him. Then you would have completely destroyed your enemy. You should have been passionate about this, but because you only did it three times, you will only win three battles but not a complete victory."

Joash didn't realize that this was a prophetic act. He didn't understand that there is a connection between the natural and the supernatural, between the visible act and the invisible world. There is a connection between what you do and what happens in the heavenlies. There is a connection between the supernatural provisions of God and your decision making, your preparation and the things that you give yourself to. You need to put forth the effort. You need to take those arrows and shoot them.

You are supposed to grab the arrows, the things in your hand and begin putting them to work, striking the ground with them. Don't stop short. Don't strike a couple of times and then back off. Don't take one business class and then say, "That's enough." Go all the way. Get your degree. Hang around those business people. Go to work for them. Keep working at it.

Most people stop short of their dreams. They do a little bit and then stop. They do a little preparation, a little prayer and a little moving in the right direction and then they stop. You have to keep going. Grab your arrows and keep striking the ground with them. Keep acting on the promises of God.

Don't stop short. Believe God to see His blessing and favor upon your life, your relationships, and your business. Believe God for the visible to line up with the invisible.

A miracle life takes a miracle-working God.

> *Men of Israel, hear these words: Jesus of Nazareth, a Man attested by God to you by miracles, wonders, and signs which God did through Him in your midst, as you yourselves also know. (Acts 2:22)*

Enlarge your concept of God. Enlarge your faith in God. Read the scriptures and begin to meditate on how great and awesome God is. Don't limit God to fit your own understanding. Author Beth Moore says, "I am utterly convinced that God is bigger than we will ever stretch our faith to conceive." [1] We put boxes around God and limit Him to someone we can understand and figure out, but He is too big to be boxed in by finite man. Take the limitations off. Take the boundaries off, not off God but off your conception of who He is. *(Mark 6:5; Exodus 15:11; Psalm 136:4)*

A miracle life takes a miracle mindset.

> *But without faith it is impossible to please Him, for he who comes to God must believe that He is, and that He is a rewarder of those who diligently seek Him. (Hebrews 11:6)*

Dee Hock, the leader of VISA, said, "The problem is never how to get new, imaginative thoughts into your mind, but how to get the old ones out. Every mind is a room packed with archaic furniture. You must get the old furniture of what you know, think and believe out before anything new can get in." [2] Move out the old furniture of disbelief and a limited view of God so you can move in the new furniture of a big God who can do all things. Clear your mind from a survival mentality and begin to put into your mind a spirit of faith for the future. Don't let anything knock you into being a failure that sees only big problems, but take your stand in the bigness of your God. *(Numbers 13:33; Matthew 6:25,32)*

A miracle life takes large prayers

> *Now this is the confidence that we have in Him, that if we ask anything according to His will, He hears us. (1 John 5:14)*

Begin to lift your prayer life up and enlarge your prayers. When Jesus was speaking with the woman at the well, He said, "If you knew who you were talking to, you would ask more than you are asking." Do you know who you are talking to? You're talking to the Almighty God. You're talking to a God who has everything at His fingertips. You're talking to a God who really loves you and who gives miracles to answer prayer. He loves to answer big prayers. *(1 Kings 2:20)*

- *Ask largely*

"Don't be so afraid of failure that you never take the step of faith, past the edge of safety, into the realm of God's mighty power."

In Alexander the Great's court, there was a philosopher who had outstanding ability but little money. He asked Alexander for financial help and was told to take whatever he needed from the imperial treasury. The man went to the treasurer and requested an amount equal to $50,000. "Absolutely not," was the response. "That's too much money to release without hearing straight from Alexander himself." When the treasurer asked Alexander, the ruler replied, "Pay the money at once. The philosopher has done me a singular honor. By the largeness of his request he shows that he has understood both my wealth and generosity." [3]

When we come to God, we need to honor Him by believing that He has the desire and the ability to answer. Too often we come asking hesitantly, unsure that God will listen and respond to our request. We can ask with confidence, knowing the balancing principle is that we must ask in accordance with His will.

- *Ask beyond the limits*

Do you remember Jabez? He was a large pray-er. He didn't limit his prayer because of his background or his upbringing or his ability. He didn't limits his prayer because of what other people thought. Remember, God's blessing for us cannot be limited by other people or by circumstances. Like Jabez, we need to live beyond the limits of our background, beyond the limits of our pain and disappointment, beyond the limits of other people's opinions.

A study was done of famous and exceptionally gifted people to understand what produced such greatness. The most outstanding fact was that virtually all of them, 392 out of 413, had to overcome very difficult obstacles in order to become who they were. [4] They were people who would not allow their situations to box them in and limit what they could accomplish.

Ask God to enlarge your territory. Live outside the fence. There are unclaimed blessings waiting for those who are willing to move beyond their own limitations and believe in a big God. *(1 Chronicles 4:9-10; Hebrews 11:1-2; Job 8:7; Jeremiah 29:11)*

A miracle life takes getting out of the boat.

> *"And Peter answered Him and said, 'Lord, if it is You, command me to come to You on the water.' So He said, 'Come.'" (Matthew 14:28-29)*

You have to take risks! A risk-free life is a victory-free life. It is boring. It is a surrender to mediocrity. You won't have to suffer big defeats, but neither will you enjoy big victories. If you are a risk-free person, you will never experience the things that God wants to do in and through you. You've got to get out of the boat. *(Matthew 14:22-33; 1 Corinthians 2:14; Mark 14:15)*

There were twelve disciples in the boat that day as it sailed across the Sea of Galilee. Twelve guys were going through the same storm and twelve guys heard Jesus say, "It is I. Don't be afraid." But only one got out of the boat. They were all looking around at the big storm and seeing the huge waves. Peter was looking at and hearing Jesus. He yelled out, "Lord, if that's really you, say the word and I'm coming." Jesus probably had a huge grin on His face as He said, "Okay, come." There were twelve guys in the boat, but only one walked on water because only one got out of the boat.

Take some risks. Get out of the boat. Don't be so afraid of failure that you never take that step of faith, past the edge of safety, into the realm of God's mighty power.

Five confessions of a miracle-driven life

Stir your faith to believe God is who He says He is. He is a miracle-working God. He is an all-powerful God who loves His children passionately and delights in seeing them live in faith. Determine to respond to His Spirit and seek His vision and goal for your life. And know that you can see the dream become reality as you live in the realm of His miraculous power.

- I have settled in my heart that God is a miracle working God, yesterday, today and forever, and He is already releasing the miracles I need for my dream.

- I pray in faith and release all the miracles God has for me: the hidden, delayed or resisted miracles. I open the door for these miracles to overtake my life.

- I know God loves me and accepts me. I have a God-given, great dream and destiny and nothing can or will stop my God-ordained future.

- I believe I will have all the miracle resources I need to accomplish my dream. There will be more than enough. I will have all I need as the occasion arises. God is my provider.

- I refuse to be limited or stopped by any obstacle, person or opinion that restricts my God-given dream. I will live my dream to the full.

Appendix

24 Imagine Scriptures

Genesis 13:14-15 "And the Lord said to Abram, after Lot had separated from him: 'Lift your eyes now and look from the place where you are— northward, southward, eastward, and westward; for all the land which you see I give to you and your descendants forever.'"

Genesis 15:1 "After these things the word of the Lord came to Abram in a vision, saying, 'Do not be afraid, Abram. I am your shield, your exceedingly great reward.'"

Genesis 28:15 "Behold, I am with you and will keep you wherever you go, and will bring you back to this land; for I will not leave you until I have done what I have spoken to you."

Genesis 37:5-6 "Now Joseph had a dream, and he told it to his brothers; and they hated him even more. So he said to them, 'Please hear this dream which I have dreamed...'"

1 Chronicles 4:10 "And Jabez called on the God of Israel saying, 'Oh, that You would bless me indeed, and enlarge my territory, that Your hand would be with me, and that You would keep me from evil, that I may not cause pain!' So God granted him what he requested."

1 Chronicles 28:20 "And David said to his son Solomon, 'Be strong and of good courage, and do it; do not fear nor be dismayed, for the Lord God—my God—will be with you. He will not leave you nor forsake you, until you have finished all the work for the service of the house of the Lord.'"

1 Kings 3:5 "At Gibeon the Lord appeared to Solomon in a dream by night; and God said, 'Ask! What shall I give you?'"

2 Kings 2:9 "And so it was, when they had crossed over, that Elijah said to Elisha, 'Ask! What may I do for you, before I am taken away from you?' Elisha said, 'Please let a double portion of your spirit be upon me.'"

Psalm 37:4 "Delight yourself also in the Lord, And He shall give you the desires of your heart."

Psalm 139:17 "How precious also are Your thoughts to me, O God! How great is the sum of them!"

Proverbs 29:18 "Where there is no revelation, the people cast off restraint; but happy is he who keeps the law."

Isaiah 41:10 "Fear not, for I am with you; Be not dismayed, for I am your God. I will strengthen you, Yes, I will help you, I will uphold you with My righteous right hand."

Isaiah 55:8-9 "'For My thoughts are not your thoughts, nor are your ways My ways,' says the Lord. 'For as the heavens are higher than the earth, so are My ways higher than your ways, and My thoughts than your thoughts.'"

Jeremiah 29:11 "For I know the thoughts that I think toward you, says the Lord, thoughts of peace and not of evil, to give you a future and a hope."

Joel 2:28 "And it shall come to pass afterward that I will pour out My Spirit on all flesh; Your sons and your daughters shall prophesy, your old men shall dream dreams, your young men shall see visions."

Habakkuk 2:2 "Then the Lord answered me and said: 'Write the vision and make it plain on tablets, that he may run who reads it.'"

Matthew 7:7-8 "Ask, and it will be given to you; seek, and you will find; knock, and it will be opened to you. For everyone who asks receives, and he who seeks finds, and to him who knocks it will be opened."

Acts 26:19 "Therefore, King Agrippa, I was not disobedient to the heavenly vision..."

1 Corinthians 2:9-10 "But as it is written: 'Eye has not seen, nor ear heard, nor have entered into the heart of man the things which God has prepared for those who love Him.' But God has revealed them to us through His Spirit. For the Spirit searches all things, yes, the deep things of God."

2 Corinthians 4:18 "While we do not look at the things which are seen, but at the things which are not seen. For the things which are seen are temporary, but the things which are not seen are eternal."

Ephesians 3:20 "Now to Him who is able to do exceedingly abundantly above all that we ask or think, according to the power that works in us..."

Philippians 3:13-14 "Brethren, I do not count myself to have apprehended; but one thing I do, forgetting those things which are behind and reaching forward to those things which are ahead, I press toward the goal for the prize of the upward call of God in Christ Jesus."

2 Timothy 1:7 "For God has not given us a spirit of fear, but of power and of love and of a sound mind."

1 John 5:14-15 "Now this is the confidence that we have in Him, that if we ask anything according to His will, He hears us. And if we know that He hears us, whatever we ask, we know that we have the petitions that we have asked of Him."

Endnotes

Chapter 1

[1] John Torre. "Lessons from Walt Disney." 2006. *Move Ahead One.* 15 Aug. 2006. (http://www.moveahead1.com/articles/article_details.asp?id=56)

[2] Charles Finney. *The Reward of Fervent Prayer.* 1850. (http://www.gospeltruth.net/1849-51Penny_Pulpit/500515pp_fervent_prayer.htm)

[3] Amit Agarwal. "Inside Bill Gates Home." 30 May 2005. *Digital Inspiration.* (http://labnol.blogspot.com/2005/05/inside-bill-gates-home.html)

[4] "T.E. Lawrence." *Wikipedia.* 11 Sep. 2006. (http://en.wikiquote.org/wiki/Thomas_Edward_Lawrence)

Chapter 2

[1] Charles F. Kettering. *Bits & Pieces.* p. 24. Dec. 1991. (http://www.sermonillustrations.com/a-z/f/faith.htm)

Chapter 3

[1] *Amplified Bible*
[2] Faiza Elmasry, "Never Too Old To Live a Dream." *Voice of America.* 28 May 2006. (http://www. voanews.com/english/archive/2006-05/2006-05-28-voa27.cfm?)

Chapter 4

[1] "American Anti Claims Silver." *ESPN.* 22 Aug. 2004. (http://sports.espn.go.com/oly/summer04/ shooting/news/story?id=1864883)

Chapter 5

[1] Trench.

Chapter 6

[1] Beth Moore. *Believing God Workbook.* (Nashville, TN: Lifeway Press, 2004) p. 32.
[2] *Sermonnotes.com.* (Alderson Press, Corporation, 2002) 2 Jan. 2002.
[3] *Today in the Word.* MBI. Aug. 1991, p. 19. Sermonillustrations.com
[4] Tim Hansel. *Holy Sweat.* 1987. (Word Books Publisher) p. 134.

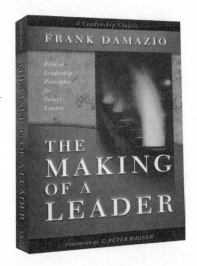

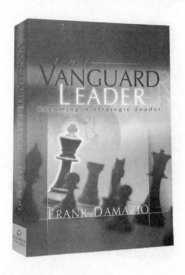

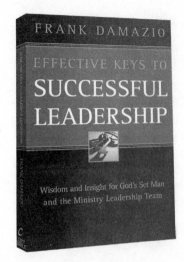

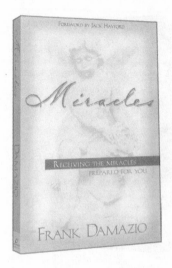

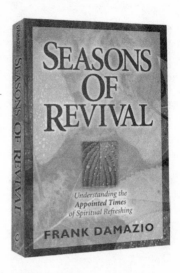

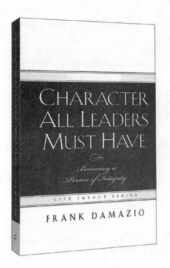

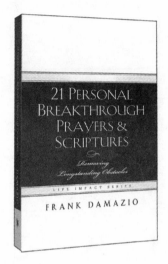

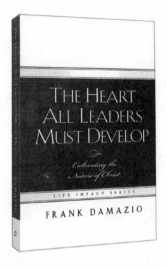

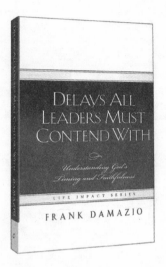